CITY CRITTERS

YOUR NEIGHBOR THE COYOTE

GREG ROZA

WINDMILL BOOKS

New York

Published in 2012 by Windmill Books, An Imprint of Rosen Publishing
29 East 21st Street, New York, NY 10010

First Edition

Editor: Jennifer Way
Layout Design: Greg Tucker

Photo Credits: Cover, pp. 4, 5, 6, 7, 13 (bottom), 16 (top, bottom), 17, 18, 20, 21, 22 Shutterstock.com; p. 8 Tom Brakefield/ Getty Images; p. 9 Steve Maslowski/Getty Images; pp. 10, 13 (top), 19 (top) iStockphoto/Thinkstock; p. 11 Tom Walker/Getty Images; p. 12 Joe McDonald/Getty Images; p. 14 Wolfgang Bayer/Getty Images; p. 15 Bob Bennett/Getty Images; p. 19 (bottom) AbleStock.com/Thinkstock.

Library of Congress Cataloging-in-Publication Data

Roza, Greg.
 Your neighbor the coyote / by Greg Roza. — 1st ed.
    p. cm. — (City critters)
 Includes index.
 ISBN 978-1-4488-5001-3 (library binding) — ISBN 978-1-4488-5131-7 (pbk.) —
 ISBN 978-1-4488-5132-4 (6-pack)
 1. Coyote—Juvenile literature. I. Title.
 QL737.C22R69 2012
 599.77'25—dc22

2011004107

Manufactured in the United States of America

For more great fiction and nonfiction, go to www.windmillbooks.com

CPSIA Compliance Information: Batch #BS2011WM: For Further Information contact Windmill Books, New York, New York at 1-866-478-0556

CONTENTS

COYOTE COUNTRY 4

NATURAL HUNTERS 6

WHAT'S FOR DINNER? 8

LIFE IN A PACK 10

COYOTE PUPS 12

IN THE WILD 14

COYOTES IN YOUR NEIGHBORHOOD 16

EASY LIVING 18

PEOPLE AND COYOTES 20

URBAN SAFARI 22

GLOSSARY 23

INDEX 24

WEB SITES 24

COYOTE COUNTRY

Just a few hundred years ago, all coyotes were animals of the wilderness. In the early 1800s, American explorers Meriwether Lewis and William Clark reported finding what they called a prairie wolf on the plains of today's Iowa and Montana.

As cities have spread across the United States, coyotes have adapted to living closer to people.

Over the next century, coyotes became a common sight in **rural** areas throughout the United States.

Today, coyotes are seen in **suburban** and **urban** areas, too. Coyotes have **adapted** to these new habitats because towns and cities are places where they can find food and shelter. This book will teach you more about how coyotes have adapted to life as a city critter.

Coyotes were once found only in rural areas. Today, coyotes are seen in suburbs and even in big cities like New York City and Chicago!

NATURAL HUNTERS

Coyotes look like medium-sized dogs. They are related to dogs and wolves. Coyotes have pointy ears and tails that hang down. Most have brownish gray coats, light-colored bellies, and bushy tails. Adults are between 32 and 37 inches (81–94 cm) long, with tails of about 16 inches (41 cm). Male coyotes are a little larger than females.

Coyotes' coats help them blend in with their surroundings. Most have brownish gray coats.

Coyotes are excellent hunters. A coyote can run about 40 miles per hour (64 km/h) for short distances and can jump about 13 feet (4 m) high. They have sharp claws and teeth for catching animals and tearing meat. They also have excellent senses of smell, vision, and hearing.

Coyotes that live farther north often have grayer coats, as this coyote in Alberta, Canada, does.

WHAT'S FOR DINNER?

In the wild, rabbits are one of the coyote's main supplies of food. However, coyotes will also eat mice, deer, bugs, and anything else they can catch. They are known to hunt **domesticated** animals, such as chickens, sheep, small cows, and pets. Coyotes sometimes hunt alone. They form packs, though, when hunting

A hungry coyote will eat whatever it can catch. This one is chasing a raccoon.

This coyote has caught a quail.

larger animals. When food is hard to find, coyotes will also eat plants and **carrion**.

Coyotes living in different places have different diets. In towns or cities, a coyote will hunt pets. Coyotes eat out of garbage cans and **compost piles**. They will also eat roadkill.

LIFE IN A PACK

Coyotes may live alone, in pairs, or in groups called packs. The pack leaders are a strong male and his **mate**. They are called the alpha male and alpha female. Other pack members may include both related and unrelated coyotes. When the alpha male and female grow old or sick, other coyotes from the pack take their places.

Here are a male (right) and a female coyote (left). Several males may try to court a female, but she will choose only one male with which to mate.

The alpha male and female are generally the only coyotes in a pack that mate. Mating season is between January and April. Male and female pairs stay together for several years. They mate once a year.

Male coyotes may fight to determine which one will be the alpha male.

COYOTE PUPS

Coyote pups are born about 63 days after mating. Most females have five or six pups. The alpha male and other members of the pack bring the mother food while the pups drink her milk. The pups first leave the den in about three or four weeks. At this point, all pack members help care for the pups.

This pup is about three weeks old. It likely is leaving its den for the first time.

Males leave the pack when they are six to nine months old. Some join new packs. Others find mates and form their own packs. Grown females generally become part of their mothers' packs.

Right: Pups greet adults by licking their mouths. That is because the adults spit up chewed food into the pups' mouths! *Bottom:* When the pups are about 10 weeks old, the mother coyote starts to teach her young how to hunt.

Coyotes may dig their own dens. They may also make dens in hollow logs, caves, and empty dens dug by other animals. They will make the dens that they take over larger, though. Coyotes communicate by using many sounds, including howls, yelps, growls, and whines. Each sound has a special meaning.

Coyote dens are often hidden from view so that the animal can rest peacefully and safely.

Coyotes in the wild live for about 6 to 8 years. About half never reach adulthood. Disease, **starvation**, and **predators** are the greatest causes of death. Life is often easier for young coyotes in towns and cities, where these things are less likely to be problems. These coyotes can live 10 to 15 years.

These pups are resting in their den.

COYOTES IN YOUR NEIGHBORHOOD

Family pets that go out at night are in danger of being eaten by coyotes.

Coyote dens may be in found in parks or woods.

Coyotes sometimes dig tunnels under fences to get at pets or livestock.

Coyote tracks look like narrow dog tracks.

Hungry coyotes sometimes raid a garden for vegetables if there are no animals to hunt.

Coyotes will check garbage cans for scraps at night.

Homeowners sometimes use loud noises, bright lights, scarecrows, and water hoses to keep coyotes away.

Coyotes can sometimes be found pulling dead animals off a road.

EASY LIVING

Urban and suburban coyotes face a different set of dangers from rural coyotes. Coyotes that live near people are more often killed by hunters, traps, and vehicles. People trying to get rid of coyotes might put out leg traps or poison for them.

However, scientists have discovered that urban and suburban coyotes have a

Coyotes try to avoid being seen. This is something that helps them survive in both urban and rural places.

greater chance of survival than rural coyotes. This is mainly because they have more food and more places to hide. Coyotes in cities and towns do not have to worry about predators such as the gray wolf, either.

Top: Coyotes risk getting hit by vehicles when they walk onto roads. This coyote is on a road in California. *Bottom:* The gray wolf, shown here, is one of the coyote's main predators.

PEOPLE AND COYOTES

Coyotes do not like being around people. Coyote attacks on people are uncommon. However, when coyotes discover a new and easy way to get food, they can grow used to people. When people leave pet food outside, coyotes may start showing up more often. This can lead to attacks, mostly on pets and small children. Most coyote attacks on people happen as they are trying to defend their pets.

This sign is warning people not to hand feed or leave food for coyotes.

Coyotes eat many pests, such as mice and squirrels. They also kill livestock and can carry diseases like rabies, though. It is important to keep your distance from coyotes because these city critters are wild animals.

Coyotes will eat pet food and sometimes pets. Feeding pets indoors and keeping them inside at night can help keep them safer.

URBAN SAFARI

It can be hard to spot coyotes in a town or city because they generally try to stay away from people. Coyotes are mostly active at night. You might see them in the early morning, though. They are often seen near roads, looking for roadkill. If you ever do see a coyote, stay far away.

You may find tracks in the morning if a coyote has passed through during the night.

You do not have to see coyotes to know that they are living in your neighborhood. On some nights, you might hear them howling to each other. They may leave behind tracks or other signs, such as damaged fences and bird feeders.

GLOSSARY

ADAPTED (uh-DAPT-ed) Changed to fit new conditions.

CARRION (KAR-ee-un) Dead, rotting flesh.

COMPOST PILES (KOM-pohst PYLZ) Piles of decaying matter, such as leaves, used as a fertilizer.

DOMESTICATED (duh-MES-tih-kayt-ed) Raised to live with people.

MATE (MAYT) A partner for making babies.

PREDATORS (PREH-duh-terz) Animals that kill other animals for food.

RURAL (RUR-ul) In the country or in a farming area.

STARVATION (star-VAY-shun) The act of suffering or dying from hunger.

SUBURBAN (suh-BER-bun) Having to do with an area of homes and businesses that is near a large city.

URBAN (UR-bun) Having to do with a city.

INDEX

C
cities, 5, 9, 15, 19, 22
coats, 6
compost piles, 9

D
dogs, 6

E
ears, 6

F
food, 5, 8–9, 12, 19–20

H
habitats, 5

hunters, 7

I
Iowa, 4

L
Lewis, Meriwether, 4
life, 5, 15

M
male(s), 10-13
Montana, 4

P
plains, 4
predators, 15, 19

S
shelter, 5
starvation, 15

T
tails, 6
teeth, 7
town(s), 5, 9, 15,
   19, 22

U
United States, 5

W
wilderness, 4
wolf, 4, 6, 19

WEB SITES

For Web resources related to the subject of this book,
go to: www.windmillbooks.com/weblinks
and select this book's title.